How to Draw
Sports

Barbara Soloff Levy

DOVER PUBLICATIONS, INC.
Mineola, New York

Note

Whether you enjoy watching sports or playing them, you'll find page after page of fun as you create thirty sports pictures using just a few simple steps. Draw a figure skater gliding across the ice, a quarterback about to throw a pass, and a surfer balancing carefully on his board, just to name a few.

To draw each figure on an instruction page, you will follow a series of steps, usually four. Begin with basic shapes such as circles in the first step. For steps two and three, add details to your pictures as shown. The last step shows you the finished drawing. It's a good idea to use a pencil with an eraser in case you want to make any changes. There are dotted lines in some of the pictures—just erase these as a final step. You'll find a helpful Practice Page opposite each instruction page, too. When you are pleased with your drawing, you may wish to go over the lines with a felt-tip pen or colored pencil. Finally, feel free to color your drawings any way you wish.

After you have finished drawing the sports figures in this book, why not use your new skills to create more drawings? It's easy!

Bibliographical Note
How to Draw Sports is a new work, first published by
Dover Publications, Inc., in 2009.

International Standard Book Number
ISBN-13: 978-0-486-47305-5
ISBN-10: 0-486-47305-8

Manufactured in the United States by RR Donnelley
47305806   2015
www.doverpublications.com

HOW TO DRAW
Sports

1

2

3

4

2   Baseball

4   Baseball

Practice Page

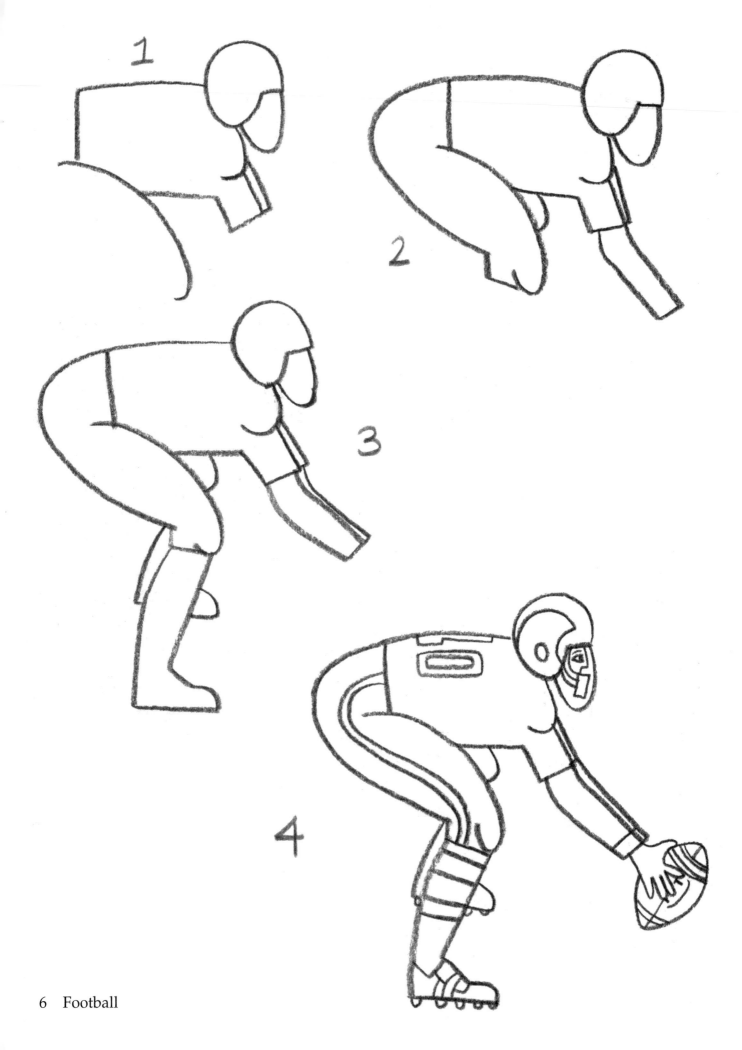

1

2

3

4

Practice Page

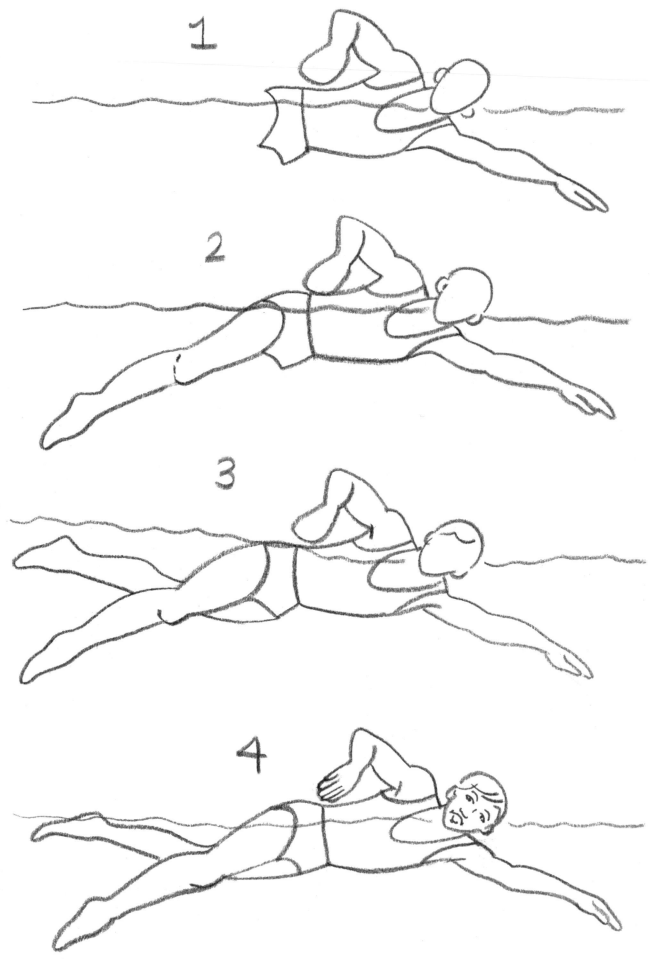

Practice Page

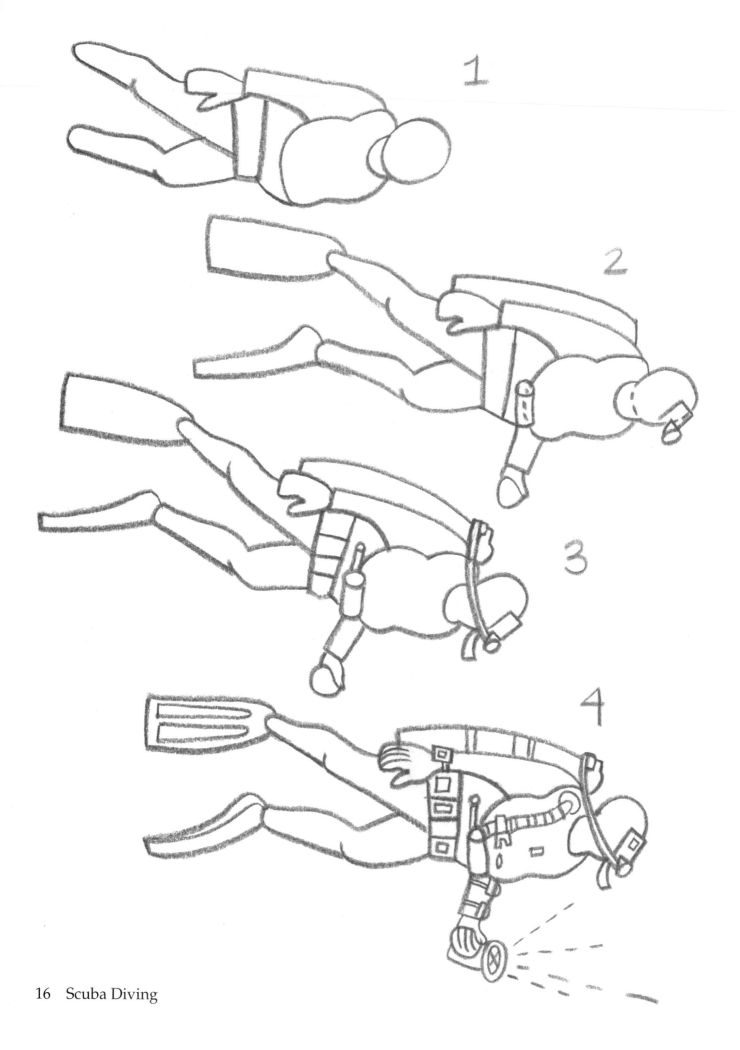

1

2

3

4

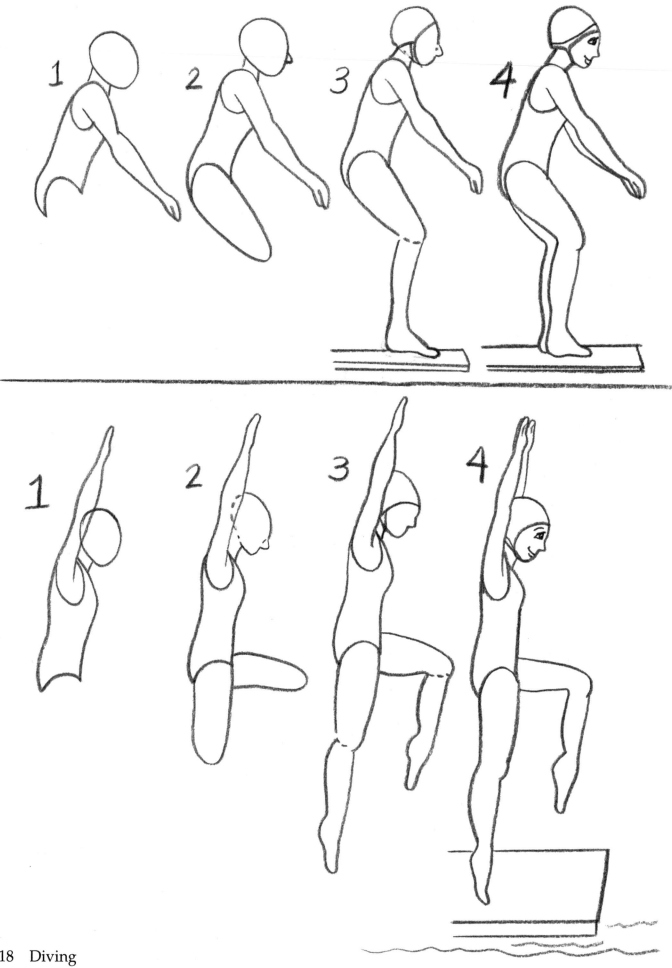

1

2

3

4

Practice Page

1

2

3

4

Practice Page

Practice Page

Practice Page

Practice Page

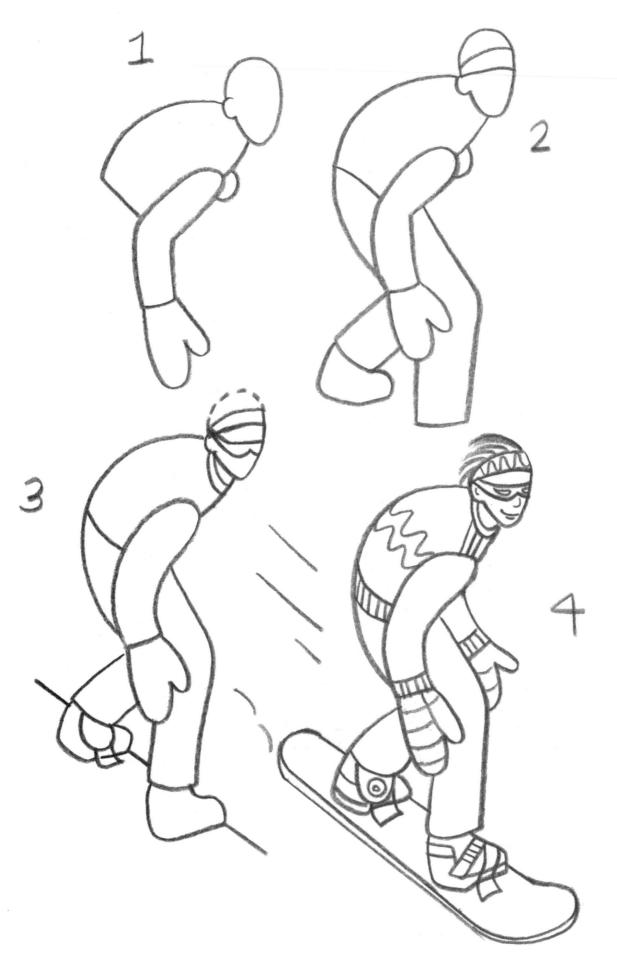

Practice Page

Practice Page

Practice Page

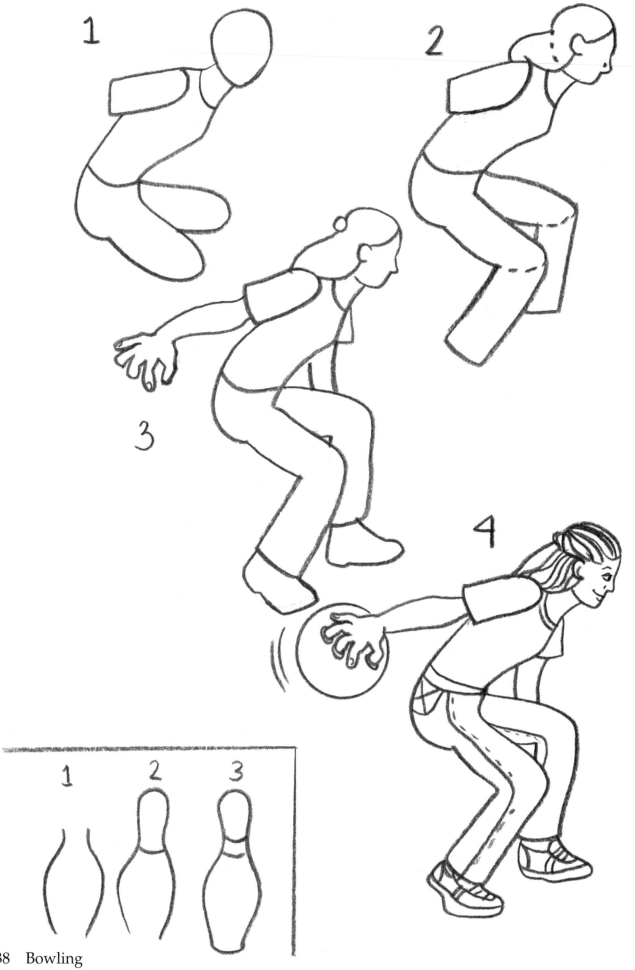

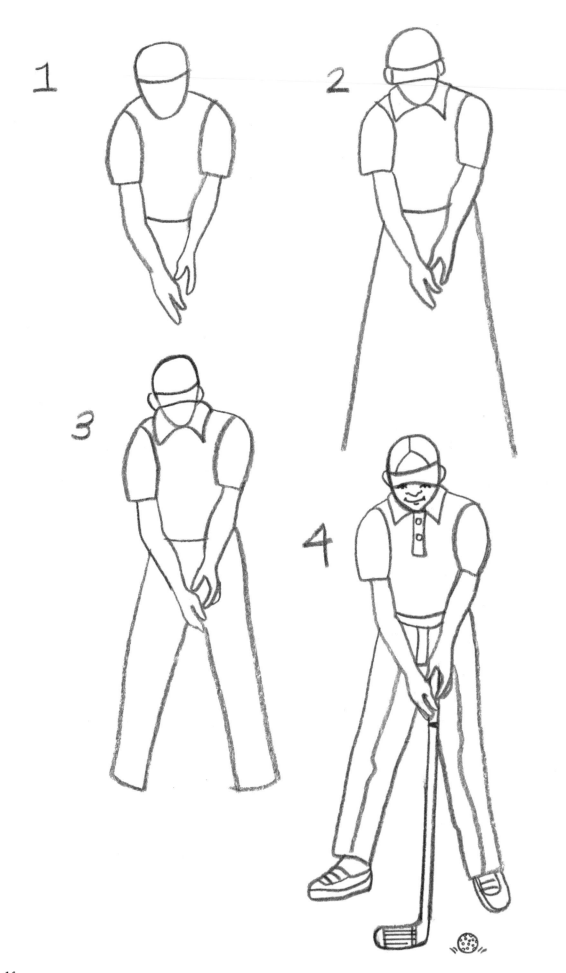

1

2

3

4

Practice Page

Practice Page

Practice Page

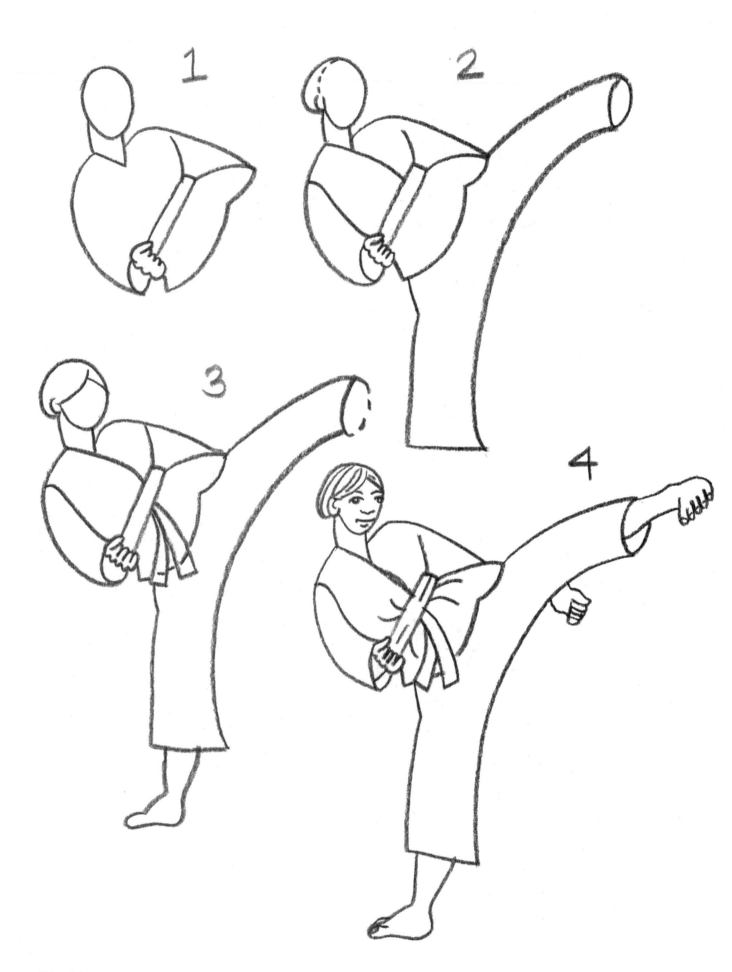